Baby's First-Year Memory Book

Lauren Rozyla

Illustrations by Kelsey Buzzell

ROCKRIDGE
PRESS

For general information on our other products and services or to obtain technical support, please contact our Customer Care Department within the United States at (866) 744-2665, or outside the United States at (510) 253-0500.

Rockridge Press publishes its books in a variety of electronic and print formats. Some content that appears in print may not be available in electronic books, and vice versa.

TRADEMARKS: Rockridge Press and the Rockridge Press logo are trademarks or registered trademarks of Callisto Media Inc. and/or its affiliates, in the United States and other countries, and may not be used without written permission. All other trademarks are the property of their respective owners. Rockridge Press is not associated with any product or vendor mentioned in this book.

Interior and Cover Designer: Linda Kocur
Art Producer: Janice Ackerman
Editor: Carolyn Abate
Production Editor: Nora Milman
Production Manager: Eric Pier-Hocking

Illustrations: ©2022 Kelsey Buzzell
Author Photo Courtesy of Justyna Harasimiuk.

Hardcover ISBN: 978-1-64876-480-6
R0

To Felicity and Ezra.
This is the baby book I was too overwhelmed
to write for either one of you!
Thank you for choosing me to be your mom.
You make me so proud every single day.

When your children arrive . . .
You realize how nice it feels
to care about someone else
more than yourself.

—AMY POEHLER, *YES PLEASE*

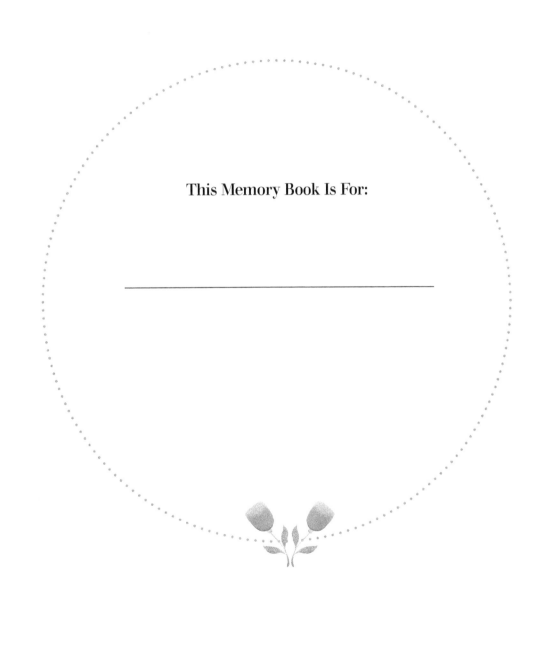

This Memory Book Is For:

_____

Introduction

Welcome to *Baby's First-Year Memory Book*, a space crafted especially for you to record the first year of your baby's life!

My name is Lauren Rozyla, and I'm a television reporter turned public relations manager. I'm also a wife and mom of two little ones who give me so much joy. Congratulations on becoming new parents. There is nothing more challenging, yet more rewarding, than raising children.

I never kept a true baby book for either of my children. This book will help you keep track of the milestones I wish I had recorded. During this process, I hope you'll be able to see just how far your baby has come, tracking their progress month by month. I also hope you'll discover all of the confidence you've gained as new parents.

Baby's First-Year Memory Book is easy to use, with simple yet engaging prompts that offer plenty of space for you to record special moments. I know each family is different and every parenting journey is unique. The prompts here allow for you to tell your own story.

Having a new baby can be incredibly overwhelming. Don't feel like you need to record everything. Just write down the moments that feel important to you whenever you can.

I hope you feel excited to begin this journey! I love to think of you sharing this book one day with your baby so they can know just how loved they've always been.

A LETTER TO WELCOME YOU

Please use this next space to say hello and welcome your baby into the world! This is also a great place to record your first thoughts and feelings about becoming a parent.

THE DAY YOU CAME HOME

Your baby is home! Now you can reflect on the last few days. Please use this next section to record what you'd like to remember.

Full name:

....

Date of birth:

....

Time of birth:

....

Place of birth:

....

Height:

....

Weight:

....

Hair color:

....

Eye color:

....

First moments:

....

....

....

....

....

....

....

PART I

Moments of
Reflection

This section is for parents to record
and reflect on the journey to parenthood.
Were you overjoyed?
Overwhelmed? There is no wrong way
to record your experience!

I came to parenting the way
most of us do—
knowing nothing and trying
to learn everything.

—MAYIM BIALIK,
ACTRESS AND NEUROSCIENTIST

WHILE PREGNANT WITH YOU

We learned we were pregnant with you when . . .

_____

_____

_____

_____

During the pregnancy, we felt . . .

_____

_____

_____

_____

The first time I felt you kick, I . . .

_____

_____

_____

_____

THE STORY BEHIND YOUR NAME

Your full name is . . .

Your name means . . .

We chose it because . . .

TELLING OUR LOVED ONES

The first people we told about you were . . .

_____

_____

_____

They reacted by . . .

_____

_____

_____

_____

They would want you to know that . . .

_____

_____

_____

_____

A NURSERY JUST FOR YOU

The theme of your nursery is . . .

....

I chose to decorate it this way because . . .

....

....

....

....

....

My favorite part of your nursery is . . .

....

....

....

....

....

YOUR BABY SHOWER

Your baby shower was hosted by . . .

_____

_____

_____

_____

The most meaningful gift we received was . . .

_____

_____

_____

_____

I felt especially happy because . . .

_____

_____

_____

_____

YOUR HOME

Your home is located . . . *(city, state, country)*

....

....

....

Your home is special because . . .

....

....

....

To us, it's important your home feels . . .

....

....

....

FAMILY HEIRLOOMS

A special keepsake in our family is . . .

_____

_____

_____

This is meaningful because . . .

_____

_____

_____

One day, I hope you will take this heirloom and . . .

_____

_____

_____

PREPARING FOR YOUR BIRTH

We got ready to welcome you by . . .

_____

_____

_____

_____

One thing we really needed was . . .

_____

_____

_____

_____

We were the most nervous that . . .

_____

_____

_____

_____

YOUR GENDER

When it came to finding out your gender, we . . .

We made that decision because . . .

When we learned your gender, we felt . . .

YOUR GRANDPARENTS

Your grandparents are . . .

_____

_____

_____

_____

One thing we want you to learn from them is . . .

_____

_____

_____

_____

We know that your grandparents . . .

_____

_____

_____

_____

ABOUT TO BE BORN

We knew I was in labor when . . .

_____

_____

_____

We got prepared for this by . . .

_____

_____

_____

One thing we wanted to have with us during labor was . . .

_____

_____

_____

WHERE YOU WERE BORN

You were born at . . .

_____

_____

_____

_____

It is located in: *(city, state, country)*

_____

_____

_____

_____

Giving birth here made us feel . . .

_____

_____

_____

_____

OUR BIRTH EXPERIENCE

We knew you would be born soon when . . .

_____

_____

_____

When giving birth, labor lasted about this long . . .

_____

_____

_____

We were so glad when . . .

_____

_____

_____

YOUR BIRTH STATISTICS

You were born weighing _____ and were

_____ inches/cm long.

The person who cut the umbilical cord is . . .

_____

_____

_____

_____

When we first heard you cry, we . . .

_____

_____

_____

_____

PRESENT DURING YOUR BIRTH

This is who was in the room:

_____

_____

_____

_____

We are grateful to . . . *(please feel free to name any doctors, nurses, doulas, midwives, and helpful family members or friends there during the birth!)*

_____

_____

_____

_____

We are glad they were there because . . .

_____

_____

_____

_____

BRINGING YOU INTO THE WORLD.

You were born via . . .

_____

_____

_____

_____

(cesarean section, vaginal birth, natural birth, water birth, surrogate, etc. are all examples!)

We had planned on . . .

_____

_____

_____

Afterward, we felt . . .

_____

_____

_____

FINALLY SEEING YOU

When we first saw you, you looked like . . .

_____

_____

_____

_____

We were surprised that . . .

_____

_____

_____

_____

We were excited to see . . .

_____

_____

_____

_____

RIGHT AFTER YOUR BIRTH

Immediately after you were born . . .

In the room, people were . . .

The big questions we had were . . .

COMING HOME

When bringing you home, we felt . . .

_____

_____

_____

_____

On the car ride home, we . . .

_____

_____

_____

_____

During the trip, you . . .

_____

_____

_____

_____

INTRODUCING YOU TO YOUR NEW HOME

The first thing we did when bringing you home was . . .

....

....

....

....

You reacted by . . .

....

....

....

....

Our loved ones made you feel welcome by . . .

....

....

....

....

YOUR FIRST NIGHT WITH US

We were the happiest after . . .

_____

_____

_____

We were the most worried when . . .

_____

_____

_____

We received help from . . .

_____

_____

_____

ANNOUNCING YOUR BIRTH

We told the world you were born by . . .

People showed they were excited about your birth by . . .

One thing everyone wanted to know is . . .

A LOOK ALL YOUR OWN

When you were born, your eye color was . . .

_____

_____

_____

_____

In terms of hair, you had . . .

_____

_____

_____

_____

We also found . . . *(note any special birthmarks or features your baby has!)*

_____

_____

_____

_____

FEEDING BABY

During mealtimes, you love to . . .

....

....

....

....

The best thing during feedings is . . .

....

....

....

The toughest part of feeding you is . . .

....

....

....

....

YOUR DAY-TO-DAY

In the morning, we typically . . .

_____

_____

_____

_____

By midday, we are ready to . . .

_____

_____

_____

_____

In the early evening, you usually . . .

_____

_____

_____

_____

SWADDLING

We learned how to swaddle you by . . .

....

....

....

....

When you're tucked in the swaddle, you . . .

....

....

....

....

Our favorite swaddling blanket is . . .

....

....

....

....

BEDTIMES AND NAPTIMES

I put you down to sleep by . . .

_____

_____

_____

You love to sleep with . . .

_____

_____

_____

I always make sure to . . .

_____

_____

_____

_____

DIAPER CHANGING

Whenever we change your diaper, we make sure to . . .

....

....

....

....

The most challenging thing about diaper changes is . . .

....

....

....

....

During diaper changes, you . . .

....

....

....

....

BATH TIME

When you are in the bath, we make sure to . . .

In the bath, you love . . .

But you really dislike . . .

BABY SELF-SOOTHING

On using a pacifier, we decided to . . .

_____

_____

_____

_____

When it comes to thumb sucking, you . . .

_____

_____

_____

To soothe yourself, you always . . .

_____

_____

_____

TUMMY TIME

We started tummy time when . . .

_____

_____

_____

_____

During tummy time, you always . . .

_____

_____

_____

_____

We were the proudest when you . . .

_____

_____

_____

_____

[PHOTO]

YOUR FIRST FRIENDS

We couldn't wait to introduce you to . . .

_____

_____

_____

You play together by . . .

_____

_____

_____

It was incredibly special when . . .

_____

_____

_____

FIRST COLD

The first time you were sick, you . . .

_____

_____

_____

_____

The first thing we did was . . .

_____

_____

_____

_____

We made you feel better by . . .

_____

_____

_____

_____

YOUR MEDICAL CARE TEAM

Your pediatrician is:

_____

_____

_____

_____

When we visit them, you . . .

_____

_____

_____

During your first checkup, we asked all about . . .

_____

_____

_____

EXPLORING IN THE STROLLER

When riding in the stroller, you . . .

_____

_____

_____

_____

One place we like to go is . . .

_____

_____

_____

One thing we look forward to on walks is . . .

_____

_____

_____

NEW CAREGIVERS

A few of our caregivers for you are . . .

_____

_____

_____

_____

We trust them with you because . . .

_____

_____

_____

_____

When we leave you with them, you . . .

_____

_____

_____

_____

LEAVING THE HOUSE

To prepare to leave the house, we always . . .

_____

_____

_____

_____

We try to make sure to bring . . .

_____

_____

_____

_____

The most challenging aspect of leaving the house is . . .

_____

_____

_____

_____

FAVORITE OUTFITS

Our favorite outfit for you is . . .

_____

_____

_____

_____

This outfit is special because . . .

_____

_____

_____

_____

When you wear it, you remind us of . . .

_____

_____

_____

_____

MOST-LOVED TOYS

You love to play with . . .

_____

_____

_____

_____

Our favorite thing to play together is . . .

_____

_____

_____

_____

We are the proudest that you . . .

_____

_____

_____

_____

CREATING A LASTING BOND

We knew you recognized us when . . .

_____

_____

_____

_____

You were about _____ months old, when this amazing experience happened.

Seeing you recognize us made me feel . . .

_____

_____

_____

_____

_____

CALMING YOUR CRIES

You get the most upset when . . .

_____

_____

_____

_____

When you seem fussy, we always make sure to . . .

_____

_____

_____

_____

When we feel overwhelmed, we turn to . . .

_____

_____

_____

_____

MAKING YOU LAUGH

We know you will laugh when we . . .

_____

_____

_____

_____

The one person who can always get you to giggle is . . .

_____

_____

_____

_____

The first time you laughed was when . . .

_____

_____

_____

_____

TEETHING AND TEARS

We know you are teething when . . .

_____

_____

_____

_____

To soothe you, we . . .

_____

_____

_____

_____

The hardest part is . . .

_____

_____

_____

_____

TRYING SOLID FOODS

You always seem to love eating . . .

_____

_____

_____

_____

One thing you'll never eat is . . .

_____

_____

_____

When trying solid foods, it was important to us that . . .

_____

_____

_____

_____

CREATING A LIFE TOGETHER

The best change we've experienced is . . .

....

....

....

The biggest adjustment to our new life is . . .

....

....

....

We want you to know that . . .

....

....

....

EXPECTATIONS VS REALITY

Before you were born, we thought . . .

_____

_____

_____

_____

However, after you were born, we learned . . .

_____

_____

_____

_____

One thing we are proud of is . . .

_____

_____

_____

_____

PLANNING FOR THE FUTURE

One thing our family hopes most for is . . .

....

....

....

....

We worry that . . .

....

....

....

....

We hope you'll always . . .

....

....

....

....

WATCHING YOU GROW

We realized you were growing when . . .

_____

_____

_____

_____

When we saw you changing so quickly, we felt . . .

_____

_____

_____

_____

One thing we can't believe is . . .

_____

_____

_____

_____

GETTING HELP

One thing we needed help with the most was . . .

_____

_____

_____

_____

There were a few people who always pitched in, including . . .

_____

_____

_____

We'll never forget how . . .

_____

_____

_____

_____

NEW PARENTHOOD

As new parents, we feel . . .

....

....

....

....

When we talk to others about being new parents, we tell them . . .

....

....

....

We wish other people understood . . .

....

....

....

....

PART II

Major Milestones

The first year of your baby's life is full of
so many happy and incredible changes.
For parents, there are so many
monumental "firsts" that show just
how far your little one has come
since entering the world.
The following section is a space
for you to record these major
milestones and what each of them
means to your family.

If you want the experience of having complete responsibility for another human being, and to learn how to love . . . then you should have children.

—MORRIE SCHWARTZ IN TUESDAYS WITH MORRIE
BY MITCH ALBOM

YOUR FIRST FEEDING

DATE

The first time we fed you, you acted . . .

During that feeding, we struggled with . . .

The first time we fed you, we were proud that . . .

The people who helped the most are . . .

THE FIRST TIME WE HELD YOU

DATE

The first time we got to hold you, we felt . . .

When in our arms, you looked like . . .

The feature we most admired in you was . . .

_____

_____

_____

_____

_____

_____

One thing you did as we held you was . . .

_____

_____

_____

_____

_____

_____

YOUR FIRST NIGHT IN THE WORLD

DATE

When putting you down to sleep, we struggled with . . .

We helped you feel safe by . . .

During the night, you often would . . .

_____

_____

_____

_____

_____

_____

That first night, we felt relieved that you . . .

_____

_____

_____

_____

_____

_____

YOUR FIRST VISITORS

DATE

_____

Your very first visitors were . . .

_____

_____

_____

_____

They were so excited to . . .

_____

_____

_____

_____

The first question they asked about you was . . .

_____

_____

_____

_____

_____

_____

During their visit, you were . . .

_____

_____

_____

_____

_____

_____

_____

_____

YOUR FIRST DIAPER CHANGES

DATE

The first person to change your diaper was . . .

When changing your diaper, they felt . . .

During those first diaper changes, we were surprised that . . .

_____

_____

_____

_____

_____

_____

During diaper changes, you handled it by . . .

_____

_____

_____

_____

_____

_____

YOUR FIRST BATH

DATE

....

Your very first bath was in . . .

....

....

....

....

To bathe you, we made sure to . . .

....

....

....

....

....

Throughout your first bath, we were the most nervous that . . .

_____

_____

_____

_____

_____

_____

During your first bath, you seemed to . . .

_____

_____

_____

_____

_____

_____

YOUR FIRST PHOTOSHOOT

DATE

[PHOTO]

Your first baby photos were taken by . . .

In the photos, you looked like . . .

For your first photos, you wore . . .

Throughout the photoshoot, you decided to . . .

YOUR FIRST CAR RIDE

DATE

We were in the car to go to . . .

Putting you into your car seat felt . . .

The person behind the wheel was ....,
and they acted . . .

_____

_____

_____

_____

_____

During the ride, you . . .

_____

_____

_____

_____

_____

_____

_____

YOUR FIRST VENTURE OUTSIDE THE HOUSE

DATE

The first time we all left the house together was to go to . . .

To make sure you had what you needed, we brought . . .

Leaving the house after you were born felt . . .

During this trip out, you mostly . . .

YOUR FIRST NAIL TRIM

DATE

We knew we needed to trim your nails when . . .

The person in charge of cutting your nails was . . .

We were the most worried that . . .

....

....

....

....

....

....

We managed to keep everyone calm by . . .

....

....

....

....

....

....

....

YOUR FIRST PLAYDATE

DATE

Your first playdate was with . . .

The main activity we did was . . .

Your first playdate was special because . . .

During that playdate, you mainly . . .

YOUR FIRST SMILE

DATE

_____

The first time you smiled, you were . . .

_____

_____

_____

_____

We knew this was a true "social smile" because . . .

_____

_____

_____

_____

_____

As parents, we felt so . . .

_____

_____

_____

_____

_____

_____

Afterward, we got you to smile again by . . .

_____

_____

_____

_____

_____

_____

_____

YOUR FIRST RUNNY NOSE

DATE

You first had a stuffy nose at the age of . . .

We were the most worried that you . . .

To help you feel better, we . . .

One thing we couldn't have done without is . . .

YOUR FIRST STROLLER RIDE

DATE

....

The first time you were in the stroller, we went . . .

....

....

....

....

....

During the ride, you mostly . . .

....

....

....

....

....

One thing we made sure to bring was . . .

_____

_____

_____

_____

_____

_____

The best thing about taking you outside was . . .

_____

_____

_____

_____

_____

_____

YOUR FIRST DAYCARE VISIT/BABYSITTER

DATE

The first time we left you in the care of someone else, we felt . . .

We got prepared by . . .

We were the most concerned that . . .

_____

_____

_____

_____

_____

_____

When we saw you at the end of the day or that evening, you . . .

_____

_____

_____

_____

_____

_____

THE FIRST TIME YOU ROLLED OVER

DATE

....

When you first rolled over, you were laying on . . .

....

....

....

....

There were signs you were getting ready to roll over because . . .

....

....

....

....

....

When we saw you roll over, we felt . . .

_____

_____

_____

_____

_____

_____

When you first flipped over, the first thing you did was . . .

_____

_____

_____

_____

_____

_____

_____

THE FIRST TIME YOU RESPONDED TO YOUR NAME

DATE

You first responded to your name at the age of . . .

When we called your name, we were surprised that you . . .

We knew you recognized your name because . . .

As parents, we felt especially . . .

YOUR FIRST CRAWL

DATE

_____

The first time you started crawling, you were . . .

_____

_____

_____

_____

We knew you were getting ready to crawl because . . .

_____

_____

_____

_____

_____

We got prepared for you to crawl by . . .

We were so proud of you because . . .

YOUR FIRST TIME SLEEPING THROUGH THE NIGHT

DATE

The first time you slept through the night, you were age:

The biggest fear we had that night was . . .

When you slept through the night, we felt . . .

The first night you slept all the way through, we were surprised that . . .

YOUR FIRST TOOTH

DATE

You got your first tooth at the age of . . .

We thought you may be getting a tooth because . . .

To help ease some of the pain, we . . .

When teething for the first time, you handled it by . . .

YOUR FIRST HAIRCUT

DATE

_____

We decided you needed a haircut when . . .

_____

_____

_____

_____

We chose to have _____ *(hairdresser, parent, caregiver)*

cut your hair because _____

_____

_____

_____

_____.

To help you stay calm during the trim, we . . .

Through the whole process, you mostly . . .

YOUR FIRST FAMILY HOLIDAY

DATE

....

Your first family holiday was . . .

....

....

....

....

On that day, we mostly just . . .

....

....

....

....

....

That day was meaningful to us because . . .

Through the celebration, you mostly . . .

YOUR FIRST FAMILY TRIP

DATE

....

Your first family trip was going to . . .

....

....

....

....

To get there, we traveled by . . .

....

....

....

....

....

We had the most fun on that trip when we . . .

_____

_____

_____

_____

_____

_____

Traveling with a new baby felt . . .

_____

_____

_____

_____

_____

_____

_____

YOUR FIRST TANTRUM

DATE

_____

This happened at the age of . . .

_____

_____

_____

_____

The reason you threw a tantrum was . . .

_____

_____

_____

_____

_____

As parents, we handled your tantrum by . . .

....

....

....

....

....

....

One thing we needed help with was . . .

....

....

....

....

....

....

....

YOUR FIRST WORD

DATE

Your first word was . . .

When we heard you say it, we . . .

Hearing you talk for the first time felt . . .

The first thing we did after you said it was . . .

YOUR FIRST SOLID FOOD

DATE

We decided to have you try solid foods at the age of . . .

The first food we introduced you to was . . .

The first time you tasted it, you . . .

_____

_____

_____

_____

_____

_____

During that taste test, we were proud that you . . .

_____

_____

_____

_____

_____

_____

_____

YOUR FIRST UNSUPPORTED SIT

DATE

The first time you sat up unsupported was at the age of . . .

While you were sitting, you were focused on . . .

Watching you, we were worried that . . .

You were able to sit up by yourself for about this long:

YOUR FIRST TIME WITH A SIPPY CUP

DATE

We first decided to introduce you to a cup when . . .

When we handed you the cup, you handled it by . . .

To teach you how to use it, we . . .

_____

_____

_____

_____

_____

We were the proudest that you managed to . . .

_____

_____

_____

_____

_____

_____

_____

YOUR FIRST STEP

DATE

You took your first step at the age of . . .

We knew you were preparing to walk because . . .

Taking those first steps, you seemed to feel . . .

The first people we told were . . .

YOUR FIRST BEST FRIEND

DATE

Your first best friend is . . .

You met them when . . .

Some special things you like to do together are . . .

_____

_____

_____

_____

_____

_____

When you are with them, you always . . .

_____

_____

_____

_____

_____

DATE

DATE

DATE

. . .

DATE

DATE

· · ·

DATE

. . .

PART III

Month-to-Month Progress

Your baby will go through
incredible changes in their first year of life.
This next section allows you to document
not just your baby's month-by-month
development but also the special moments
that you as parents will never
want to forget. Years from now,
your family can look back on how
you grew together.

There is no such thing
as a perfect parent
so just be a real one.

—SUE ATKINS, TELEVISION PRESENTER
AND PARENTING COACH

MONTH:

....

DATE:

....

HEIGHT:

....

WEIGHT:

....

YOUR FAVORITE THINGS:

....

....

....

....

IMPORTANT "FIRSTS" THIS MONTH:

....

....

HOW YOU'VE CHANGED FROM LAST MONTH:

....

....

WHAT I'M LOOKING FORWARD TO NEXT MONTH:

....

....

MY MEMORIES FROM THIS MONTH:

....

....

....

....

MONTH:

_____

DATE:

_____

HEIGHT:

_____

WEIGHT:

_____

YOUR FAVORITE THINGS:

_____

_____

_____

_____

IMPORTANT "FIRSTS" THIS MONTH:

....

....

HOW YOU'VE CHANGED FROM LAST MONTH:

....

....

WHAT I'M LOOKING FORWARD TO NEXT MONTH:

....

....

MY MEMORIES FROM THIS MONTH:

....

....

....

....

MONTH:

....

DATE:

....

HEIGHT:

....

WEIGHT

....

YOUR FAVORITE THINGS:

....

....

....

....

IMPORTANT "FIRSTS" THIS MONTH:

....

....

HOW YOU'VE CHANGED FROM LAST MONTH:

....

....

WHAT I'M LOOKING FORWARD TO NEXT MONTH:

....

....

MY MEMORIES FROM THIS MONTH:

....

....

....

....

....

MONTH:

....

DATE:

....

HEIGHT:

....

WEIGHT:

....

YOUR FAVORITE THINGS:

....

....

....

....

IMPORTANT "FIRSTS" THIS MONTH:

....

....

HOW YOU'VE CHANGED FROM LAST MONTH:

....

....

WHAT I'M LOOKING FORWARD TO NEXT MONTH:

....

....

MY MEMORIES FROM THIS MONTH:

....

....

....

....

....

MONTH:

....

DATE:

....

HEIGHT:

....

WEIGHT:

....

YOUR FAVORITE THINGS:

....

....

....

....

IMPORTANT "FIRSTS" THIS MONTH:

_____

_____

HOW YOU'VE CHANGED FROM LAST MONTH:

_____

_____

WHAT I'M LOOKING FORWARD TO NEXT MONTH:

_____

_____

MY MEMORIES FROM THIS MONTH:

_____

_____

_____

_____

_____

MONTH:

_____

DATE:

_____

HEIGHT:

_____

WEIGHT

_____

YOUR FAVORITE THINGS:

_____

_____

_____

_____

Baby's First-Year Memory Book

IMPORTANT "FIRSTS" THIS MONTH:

....

....

HOW YOU'VE CHANGED FROM LAST MONTH:

....

....

WHAT I'M LOOKING FORWARD TO NEXT MONTH:

....

....

MY MEMORIES FROM THIS MONTH:

....

....

....

....

MONTH:

DATE:

HEIGHT:

WEIGHT:

YOUR FAVORITE THINGS:

IMPORTANT "FIRSTS" THIS MONTH:

....

....

HOW YOU'VE CHANGED FROM LAST MONTH:

....

....

WHAT I'M LOOKING FORWARD TO NEXT MONTH:

....

....

MY MEMORIES FROM THIS MONTH:

....

....

....

....

MONTH:

....

DATE:

....

HEIGHT:

....

WEIGHT:

....

YOUR FAVORITE THINGS:

....

....

....

....

IMPORTANT "FIRSTS" THIS MONTH:

....

....

HOW YOU'VE CHANGED FROM LAST MONTH:

....

....

WHAT I'M LOOKING FORWARD TO NEXT MONTH:

....

....

MY MEMORIES FROM THIS MONTH:

....

....

....

....

MONTH:

....

DATE:

....

HEIGHT:

....

WEIGHT:

....

YOUR FAVORITE THINGS:

....

....

....

....

IMPORTANT "FIRSTS" THIS MONTH:

....

....

HOW YOU'VE CHANGED FROM LAST MONTH:

....

....

WHAT I'M LOOKING FORWARD TO NEXT MONTH:

....

....

MY MEMORIES FROM THIS MONTH:

....

....

....

....

MONTH:

....

DATE:

....

HEIGHT:

....

WEIGHT:

....

YOUR FAVORITE THINGS:

....

....

....

....

IMPORTANT "FIRSTS" THIS MONTH:

....

....

HOW YOU'VE CHANGED FROM LAST MONTH:

....

....

WHAT I'M LOOKING FORWARD TO NEXT MONTH:

....

....

MY MEMORIES FROM THIS MONTH:

....

....

....

....

MONTH:

....

DATE:

....

HEIGHT:

....

WEIGHT:

....

YOUR FAVORITE THINGS:

....

....

....

....

IMPORTANT "FIRSTS" THIS MONTH:

....

....

HOW YOU'VE CHANGED FROM LAST MONTH:

....

....

WHAT I'M LOOKING FORWARD TO NEXT MONTH:

....

....

MY MEMORIES FROM THIS MONTH:

....

....

....

....

MONTH:

DATE:

HEIGHT:

WEIGHT:

YOUR FAVORITE THINGS:

IMPORTANT "FIRSTS" THIS MONTH:

....

....

HOW YOU'VE CHANGED FROM LAST MONTH:

....

....

WHAT I'M LOOKING FORWARD TO NEXT MONTH:

....

....

MY MEMORIES FROM THIS MONTH:

....

....

....

....

YOUR FIRST BIRTHDAY

This is such a joyous and wonderful occasion! Please use the next few lines to share what stood out about your little one's first birthday.

We celebrated your first birthday by . . .

....

....

....

The loved ones who came to celebrate with you were . . .

....

....

....

Your favorite gifts were . . .

....

....

....

On your birthday, we felt so proud you were able to . . .

....

....

....

As parents, your first birthday felt bittersweet because . . .

....

....

....

One thing we'll always remember about your first birthday is . . .

....

....

....

A LETTER TO YOU ON YOUR FIRST BIRTHDAY

This is a space for you to look back on your baby's first year, celebrate their first birthday, and preserve important memories about this special time.

Embrace your beautiful mess
of a life with your child.
No matter how hard it gets,
do not disengage.
Do something—anything—to
connect with and guide
your child today.
Parenting is an adventure
of the greatest significance.
It is your legacy.

—ANDY KERCKHOFF

References

"10 Inspiring Quotes for Your First Year of Parenting." Gender Reveal. March 2, 2017. GenderReveal.com/10-inspiring-quotes-for-your-first-year-of-parenting.

Albom, Mitch. *Tuesdays with Morrie*. 10th ed. New York: Broadway Books, 2007.

Atkins, Sue. "Because Kids Don't Come with a Handbook!" Sue Atkins. April 13, 2011. SueAtkinsParentingCoach.com/2011/04/because-kids-dont-come-with-a-handbook.

Bongiorno, Kim. "40 Best Parenting Quotes of All Time." Momtastic. July 16, 2020. Momtastic.com/parenting/541137-40-amazing-quotes-parenthood.

Poehler, Amy. *Yes Please*. New York: Dey St., 2018.

About the Author

 **Lauren Rozyla** spent 10 years as an Emmy-award winning television journalist and now serves as a public relations manager in city government. Life changed dramatically for her when she became a new mother. A survivor of postpartum anxiety and depression, she now works to tackle the stigma of mental health issues and motherhood. She lives in Tampa with her wonderful husband, daughter, and son, alongside her beloved flock of backyard chickens. Feel free to connect with her on social media at @laurenrozyla.

CPSIA information can be obtained
at www.ICGtesting.com
Printed in the USA
JSHW030844010222
22452JS00001B/1